P9-DDV-055

Ian McEwan

The Cement Garden

Adapted by David Aula and Jimmy Osborne

B L O O M S B U R Y

LONDON · NEW DELHI · NEW YORK · SYDNEY

Bloomsbury Methuen Drama

An imprint of Bloomsbury Publishing Plc

50 Bedford Square	1385 Broadway
London	New York
WC1B 3DP	NY 10018
UK	USA

www.bloomsbury.com

Bloomsbury is a registered trade mark of Bloomsbury Publishing Plc

The Cement Garden by Ian McEwan

Adapted for the stage by David Aula and Jimmy Osborne

The Cement Garden was first published in 1978
by Jonathan Cape and by Vintage in 1997

© Ian McEwan, David Aula and Jimmy Osborne

This stage adaptation first published in 2014 by Bloomsbury Methuen Drama

Ian McEwan, David Aula and Jimmy Osborne have asserted their
rights under the Copyright, Designs and Patents Act, 1988, to be
identified as authors of this work.

All rights reserved. No part of this publication may be reproduced or
transmitted in any form or by any means, electronic or mechanical,
including photocopying, recording, or any information storage or retrieval
system, without prior permission in writing from the publishers.

No responsibility for loss caused to any individual or organization
acting on or refraining from action as a result of the material in
this publication can be accepted by Bloomsbury or the author.

All rights whatsoever in this play are strictly reserved and application for
performance etc. should be made before rehearsals begin by professionals and
amateurs to MacFarlane Chard Associates, 33 Percy Street, London W1T 2DE.
No performance may be given unless a licence has been obtained.

No rights in incidental music or songs contained in the work are hereby
granted and performance rights for any performance/presentation
whatsoever must be obtained from the respective copyright owners.

British Library Cataloguing-in-Publication Data
A catalogue record for this book is available from the British Library.

ISBN: PB: 978-1-4725-8383-3

Library of Congress Cataloging-in-Publication Data
A catalog record for this book is available from the Library of Congress.

Typeset by Mark Heslington Ltd, Scarborough, North Yorkshire
Printed and bound in Great Britain

Heritage Arts Company presents
FallOut Theatre's production of

THE CEMENT GARDEN

BY IAN McEWAN

ADAPTED BY **DAVID AULA**
AND **JIMMY OSBORNE**

First performed as part of the VAULT Festival, 28 January–8 March, 2014 as a FallOut Theatre Production presented by the Heritage Arts Company

CAST

David Annen as Tom
Ruby Bentall as Julie
Georgia Clarke-Day as Sue
Victoria Gould as Mother
George MacKay as Jack
Christopher Webster as Derek/Father/Commander Hunt

CREATIVE TEAM

Directed by **David Aula**
Designed by **Georgia de Grey**
Lighting Design by **Stuart Webb**
Sound Design by **Edward Lewis**
Stage Manager **Sarah Wilson**
Production Manager **Clíona Ní Mhocháin**
Produced by **Mat Burt** for the Heritage Arts Company

VAULT Festival | www.thevaultfestival.com

Produced by	The Heritage Arts Company
Festival Co-Directors	Tim Wilson & Mat Burt
Production Manager	Andy George
Assistant Production Manager	Clíona Ní Mhocháin
Production Coordinator	Jessica Hall
Front of House Manager	Cassandra Mills
Financial Controller	Bob Thomas
Production Accountant	Dee Vithlani

FallOut Theatre | www.fallouttheatre.com

Artistic Director	David Aula
Writer In Residence	Jimmy Osborne
Artistic Associates	Jack Monaghan, Patrick Warner & Rebecca Pitt
Lighting Designer	David Mack
Producers	Ollie Jordan & James Baggaley

The Heritage Arts Company | www.heritagearts.co.uk

Creative Producer	Tim Wilson
Creative Director	Mat Burt
Head of Production	Andy George

Jimmy Osborne:

For Mum, Dad and Our Kid – thank you.

Thanks: Ian McEwan, all at FallOut Theatre, Heritage Arts, the Eagle, Julie Press, Anna Brewer and the Peggy Ramsay Foundation.

David Aula:

For Abigail, Bex, Hannah, Jack, Kate and Paddy.

Thanks: I would also like to thank all those on Jimmy's list. And I'd like to add Miles Cherry, Nick Bampos, Martin and Claire Daunton, Jeremy Hardingham, The National Theatre Studio, The Park Theatre, Nick Quinn, Robert Taylor, David Birley and Sally Carr. To James and Ollie for keeping the dream alive and to Mat for helping me rediscover my mojo. Caitlin for your belief, your support, and your laugh: thank you.

The Cement Garden

Characters

Father
Mother
Julie, *fifteen at the start.*
Jack, *thirteen at the start.*
Sue, *eleven at the start.*
Tom, *four at the start.*
Older Tom, *late forties.*
Derek, *twenty-three.*
Commander Hunt

N.B. When **Jack** *'narrates' he is talking to* **Older Tom**.

Prologue

The Family Home

Older Tom *searches through the remains of the house and 'finds'* **Jack** . . .

Jack (*to* **Older Tom**)   I did not kill our father, but sometimes I felt that I had helped him on his way. And but for the fact that it coincided with a landmark in my own physical growth, his death seemed insignificant compared with what followed. I am only including the little story of his death to explain how our sisters and I came to have such a large quantity of cement at our disposal.

Cellar

Father *and* **Mother**

A large, old army chest and a cot.

A pile of cement bags lies under the coal chute.

Father *struggles to move the cement bags into an ordered pile.*

Mother   Cement?

Father   Fifteen bags.

Mother   For?

Father   Fifteen bags all present and correct.

Mother   What's it for?

Father (*out of breath*)   For . . . the garden.

Mother   The . . . what's wrong with plants?

Father   Neater.

Mother   But cement?

Father   Nothing growing where it shouldn't.

Mother   Everywhere cement?

Father   Everything in its place.

Mother   I don't want to look out of the kitchen window and see a car park.

Father (*deep breaths*)   It'll be . . . tidier . . . I won't be able to keep up the garden now, with my (*Pats his heart.*).

Mother   But now you've recovered . . . you love that garden.

Father   . . . and it'll keep the muck off your clean floors . . .

Mother   It's the only green for miles, now we've got the motorway, thundering –

Father   . . . and it would be easier for you if you end up on your –

Mother   – how much did it all cost?

Father   Never you mind.

Mother   Have you checked the Post Office account this month?

Father (*laughs*)   I suppose you have? That'll be (*Laughter turns to coughing.*), that'll be reliable.

Enter **Tom**.

Mother   Tom starts school in September.

Father   Good.

Mother   He'll need a uniform, pens, books.

Father   What that boy needs is (*Lost in more coughing.*) . . .

Mother   Where's the money going to come from?

Father   It's here now – fifteen bags. I can't exactly . . .

Mother   Send it back.

Father   All signed for.

Mother   Send it back.

Father   Out of the question.

Mother   We can't afford it.

Father   There's nothing to be done.

Father *finishes moving the bags.*

Mother   Send it back.

Father   It's out of the question!

Mother   Where will the children play?

Father   That's the end of it, woman

Mother   Please. Send it back.

Father   Out of the question!

Jack's Bedroom

Sue *is upset by the parents' argument downstairs.* **Jack** *and* **Julie** *distract her with a game.*

Julie   Ve must prepare the specimen for investigation!

Sue *lies on the bed.*

Jack (*examining* **Sue**)   Hmmm, vot do you think it is, Fräulein?

Julie   Something, a creature, from outer space.

Father (*off*)   That's the end of it!

Jack   Ja, intriguing.

Julie   I vill point your attention, Herr Doktor, to the specimen's unusually large and unusually beautiful eyes; its unusually slender neck, Herr Doktor, and it's impressive but unusually large cranium.

Jack   Ah yes, unusually – impressively unusually – large for a specimen of this –

Julie   – you vill also notice these very unusual markings on the creature's face . . . millions of tiny little markings . . .

Sue   Julie, don't!

Julie   I think ze only thing to do, Herr Doktor, is to examine further. Ve must remove ze outer shell.

Jack   Sterilise ze instruments!

*They remove **Sue**'s clothes.*

Julie   You will see, Herr Doktor, ze skin clinging tightly to ze ribcage.

Jack   Bring ze lights!

Julie   Zat is a fine example of highly muscular buttocks!

Jack   See how zey resemble ze shoulder blades. Unusual.

Sue *squeals loudly in delight.*

Julie   Ze specimen is trying to alert ze mother ship!

Jack   Nurse, I need to investigate where ze sound is coming from.

Julie   Is zere anything you can do, Herr Doktor!?

Jack   Perhaps if I remove ze tongue . . . ?

Sue   I'll stop! I've stopped! I'll be quiet, I promise.

*Enter **Tom**, unnoticed. He watches.*

*They open **Sue**'s legs and examine her with the torch.*

Julie   And, vot do you think of zis Herr Doktor?

Jack *and* **Julie** *look at each other for a moment, waiting for the other to go first.*

Jack (*to* **Older Tom**)   We found the little flower made of flesh. But I was looking at Julie: she had a high ridge of cheekbone beneath her eyes, which gave her the deep look of some rare wild animal. She glanced at me. We looked at each other knowingly, knowing nothing.

Julie *moistens her finger and strokes* **Sue** *between her legs.*

Jack *moistens his finger and slides it over* **Julie***'s finger.*

Julie   Nothing serious.

Sue (*whispers*)   Don't stop, please!

Julie   But we will watch for further developments, ja?

Sue   Carry on! Carry on!

Jack   Julie.

Julie   It's your turn.

Jack   I'll examine you.

Sue   Please, Julie!

Julie   It's Jack's turn, Sue.

Jack   Out of the question!

Julie   Come on, Jack.

Jack   That's the end of it!

Jack *throws* **Sue***'s skirt at* **Julie***.*

Tom   Mum said it's dinner time.

Dining Room & Bathroom

Jack *masturbates in the bathroom.*

Julie *and* **Sue** *are setting the table in the dining room.*

Jack *enters the dining room and sits at the table.*

Mother *enters with dinner and* **Tom***.*

Mother   Jack. Jack.

Julie (*smirks*)   What were you doing in the bathroom?

Mother   Help your sisters with the table. Make sure the cloth is nice and straight; you know your father likes a tidy table.

Table ready, they all sit.

Mother (*calls*)   Father, dinner!

They wait, and wait.

Enter **Father** – *he sits at the head of the table.*

Jack (*to* **Older Tom**)   Dinner was father's favourite time . . .

Jack *passes* **Father**'*s plate to him.*

Father   Keep my dinner away from your spotty face.

Everyone but **Jack** *laughs ritually.*

Father   Tom, sit up straight at the table!

Mother   Don't.

Tom   Don't!

Julie   Father, will you come to the sports meeting on Saturday?

Father   I don't think so.

Julie   Please.

Father   It's daft, a girl running.

Everyone but **Julie** *laughs.*

Jack   Julie's bound to win.

Father   No.

Sue   She always wins.

Jack   We'll be waiting at the finish line.

Sue   Cheering!

Father   Susan, do you ever brush your hair? You look like an alien.

Everyone but **Sue** *forces laughter.*

Mother   Julie's running in the 100-yard sprint.

Father   And you can count that high, can you?

Everyone but **Mother** *barely laughs.*

Mother   And the 220-yard –

Father   – Tom, pay attention to your mother!

Mother   *He* was.

Tom   He was!

Father *uses his knife to clean out his pipe bowl, emptying it over his dinner.*

Father   Tonight, Tom, try not to wet the bed again.

Tom *buries his head in* **Mother**'s *arms.*

Cellar

Tom *is rooting through old family stuff.*

Julie *and* **Jack** *sit on the army trunk.*

Jack   Tom, stop making a mess – Father will be angry.

Tom   Don't care. Mum says not to listen.

Jack   Just decide which toys you're taking up.

Tom   None. This stuff's for babies.

Jack   Put it away, then.

Tom   Gonna find some good things.

Tom *continues his search.*

Julie   How come jokes are not made about Father?

Jack   Because jokes about Father are not funny.

Julie   Really?

Jack   Out of the question!

Julie   Then what does Father do when he has a problem with constipation?

Jack   I have no idea, what does Father do when he has a problem with constipation?

Julie   He works it out with a pencil!

They fall about laughing. **Tom** *comes over dragging his old cot.*

Tom   Take this upstairs for me, spotty puss head!

Jack   Piss off, what do you want that for?

Tom   To sleep in.

Julie   Tom, don't be silly, put it back . . .

Jack   Wait, wait! I've got one, I've got one.

Julie   Tell me!

Jack (*clears his throat*)   I saw something in the garden the other day that gave me a shock.

Julie   Oh yes, what was that?

Jack   A flower.

Julie   Brilliant!

They laugh.

Tom   Jaaack, do it for me.

Jack   No, how about I smash it up instead?!

Tom   No don't! Don't!

Jack   Who's the baby now? Crying over your cot.

Tom *runs off.*

Tom   Mum!

Julie *giggles.*

Julie   Now you're for it.

Jack   We'll do the joke at dinner time tomorrow.

Julie   Father'll have to laugh now.

They shake hands.

Garden

Mother, Father, Jack *and* **Julie**

Mother   Apologise to your father.

Julie   But –

Mother   That was quite unnecessary at dinner.

Jack   What was?

Mother   Apologise.

Pause – **Father** *cleans his pipe.*

Julie   Sorry.

Mother   Jack. Jack.

Pause.

Father *holds out his hand.* **Jack** *goes to shake it.*

Father   Gloves. We're mixing cement.

Jack *passes* **Father** *his work gloves.*

Exit **Mother** *and* **Julie**.

Father *and* **Jack** *work. They bend to pick up a bag of cement. Each waits for the other to lift first.*

Jack   One, two, three!

Father *lifts,* **Jack** *delays, letting* **Father** *take the strain and then he too lifts. They carry the bag across the garden.*

Jack   Can you manage?

Father   Of course . . . of course I can . . . manage.

Jack   I could take more weight if you can't.

Father   No, no, I . . .

They lift another bag, again **Jack** *delays.*

Jack   It's a great idea. It'll be a great place to play football, or for helicopters to land.

Father (*breathing hard*)   Shovel.

Jack *passes* **Father** *the shovel.* **Father** *splits one of the bags with it and starts to mix the cement.*

They work.

Father   Not like that.

They work.

Father   Use the inside of your knee, boy.

Jack *tries.*

Father   No, against your forearm.

Jack *tries.*

Father   That's it. Better leverage.

Jack *tries.*

Father   Oh give it here.

Jack *puts his hand in his pants.*

Jack   Where are Sue and Julie, why aren't they helping?

Father   Let's get, let's get (*Wipes his brow.*), let's get on.

Jack   I need to go to the toilet.

Father   Be quick, boy.

Jack (*to* **Older Tom**)   In the bathroom I worked on myself rapidly. As usual, the image before me was Julie's hand between Sue's legs. Then it happened.

Father *collapses face first on to the cement.*

Jack   Then it happened, it appeared on my hand, it appeared quite suddenly on the back of my wrist, and though I knew about it from jokes and school biology books, and had been waiting for many months, now I was astonished and moved. Against the downy hairs, lying across the edge of a concrete stain, glistened a little patch of liquid, not milky as I had thought, but colourless.

Jack *sniffs his hand. Dabs at it with his tongue.*

Jack   As I watched, it dried to a barely visible crust. I decided not to wash it away.

Jack *notices his* **Father** *face down. Looks at him for some time.*

Jack   I did not kill our father.

But sometimes I felt I had helped him along the way.

Jack looks at the imprint of his **Father**'s *face in the concrete.*

Act One

Bathroom

Jack (*to* **Older Tom**)   By the time a year had passed since Father's death, my spots were so thoroughly established across my face that I abandoned all the rituals of personal hygiene. I no longer washed my face or hair or cut my nails or took baths. I gave up brushing my teeth. I felt insulated in the layer of grease across my skin.

Jack *looks at himself in the mirror. Strikes a heroic pose.*

Mother   I've put some clean clothes out for you.

Jack   If people really like me, they will take me as I am.

Mother   Of course.

Jack   It doesn't matter what anybody else says.

Mother   That's right.

Jack   I can say anything I like.

Mother   Of course, Jack.

Jack   Tough . . .

Mother   I'm so proud of you

Jack   . . . tough . . .

Mother   So very, very –

Jack   . . . shit . . .

Mother   – proud.

Jack   . . . shit . . .

Mother   My son Jack.

Jack   . . . piss . . . piss . . .

Enter **Sue**.

Jack   . . . ARSE . . .

Sue   What are you doing?

Jack   Nothing.

Jack *looks to* **Mother** – *she's not there.*

Jack   Nothing.

Sue   Who were you talking to?

Jack   What do you want?

Sue   I needed something from the cabinet.

Jack   What?

Sue   I'll get it later.

Jack   I'll get it for you.

Sue   No, honestly.

Jack   You mean this lotion?

Sue   Give it back.

Jack   For dissolving freckles?

Sue   Julie doesn't want to walk to school with you this morning.

Jack   Why not?

Sue   I don't know.

Jack   Why not, we always walk to school?

Sue   I don't know.

Jack   I'll walk to school with her anyway.

Sue   She'll run off.

Jack   I'll run after her.

Sue   You think you can catch her?

Jack   Yes.

Sue   She's still got the under-eighteen 100-yard record, you know.

Jack   Girls' under-eighteen 100-yard record.

Sue   All the boys flock round her at school. She could outrun any one of them. If she wanted to. She's got loads of boyfriends.

Jack   She never lets any of them get near her.

Sue   All the girls want to be her. The rebellious ones. The girls Mum says have 'reputations'.

Jack   How does Mum know – no one ever comes to the house?

Sue   It's because she wears petticoats beneath her skirts so they swirl when she turns.

Jack   And stockings and black knickers.

Beat.

Sue   Do you think I could wear them?

Jack   Stockings?

Sue   Yes, and black knickers?

Jack   You?

Enter **Julie** *and* **Tom**.

Jack   You're too busy dissolving freckles.

Sue *exits.*

Julie   Mum says you're to take Tom today.

Jack   No she didn't, you're making it up.

Julie   Mum's too tired to do it. She's drained. Spare her the walk.

Jack   Why don't you do it, if you're that bothered?

Julie   I've got to leave now, and Tom's not ready.

Jack   I've got to leave now, too.

Julie   Take him.

Exit **Julie**.

Beat.

Jack (*calls*)   Sue, Mum says you're to take Tom to school, don't forget!

Jack *runs after* **Julie**, *leaving* **Tom**.

Sue (*off*)   What! No! Wait.

Enter **Sue** *and* **Tom**.

Sue (*sighs*)   Come on then, we haven't got all day.

Tom   Not going freckle face, not going!!

Street

Julie *walking*.

Jack (*to* **Older Tom**)   Julie could run like the wind, but walked as though asleep, slowly and in a very straight line. She appeared deep in thought, but when asked always protested that her mind was empty. She lived in the separate world of those who are, and secretly know they are, exceptionally beautiful.

Jack *runs after her and tries to grab* **Julie**'s *wrist*.

Jack   Carry your satchel, miss.

Julie *pulls away*.

Jack   Wanna race?

Julie *keeps walking*.

Jack   Wanna fight?

Julie *ignores him*.

Jack   What's wrong with you?

Julie   Nothing.

Jack   Are you pissed off?

Julie   Yes.

Jack   With me?

Julie   Yes.

Jack *stops*.

Jack   Because of Mum? What, isn't she sleeping?

Julie *walks away*.

Jack   I'll go back then.

Julie *exits*. **Jack** *watches her go*.

Enter **Sue***, dragging* **Tom**.

Sue   I thought you had to rush off.

Tom   Had to rush off. Stinky.

Jack *makes to hit* **Tom**. **Tom** *hides behind* **Sue**.

Sue   You're going to be late.

Jack   Forgot something.

Tom   Don't want to go.

Sue   Come on, Tom.

Jack   I caught up with Julie.

Tom   Don't want to go! I don't like it!

Sue   Where is she then?

Jack   I let her go.

Sue   Tom, we'll be late.

Sue *drags* **Tom** *off*.

Jack *walks back to the house*.

Jack (*to* **Older Tom**)   I walked round the side of the house to the back garden and watched Mother through one of the kitchen windows.

Mother *is clearing up breakfast. She takes a pill from a bottle.*

Jack (*to* **Older Tom**)   I was struck by the obvious fact of her independent existence; she went on even when I was away. She was not a particular invention of mine or of our sisters, though I continued to invent and ignore her.

Mother *notices* **Jack***.*

Mother   Jack?

Mother *opens her arms to* **Jack***.*

Jack *runs away.*

Mother   Jack!

Jack!

Mother *becomes a creature from outer space – chasing* **Jack** *through his dreams.*

Jack's Bedroom

Another day.

Jack *is asleep.* **Mother** *is sat on* **Jack***'s bed.*

Mother   Jack.

Jack.

Jack.

Jack *wakes with a start.*

Pause.

Mother   It's time we had a talk you and I.

Jack   It's half past eight, I'll be –

Mother   – you lie there a moment.

Jack   I'm going to be late, Julie will be gone.

Mother   You lie there a moment. I want to talk to you.

Look at me, I want to look at your eyes.

Have you looked at your eyes in the mirror lately?

Jack   No.

Mother   Your pupils are very large, did you know that?

Jack *shakes his head.*

Mother   And there are bags under your eyes, even though you've just woken up.

Beat.

Mother   Do you know why that is?

Jack *shakes his head.*

Mother   You know what I'm talking about, don't you?

Jack (*quietly*)   No.

Mother   Yes, yes you do, my boy. You know what I'm talking about . . . I can see you do.

Beat.

Mother   Don't think I don't know what's going on. You're . . . you're growing into a young man now, and I'm very proud you are . . . these are things your father would have been telling you.

Jack   Dad?

Mother   Growing up is difficult, but if you carry on the way you are, you're going to do yourself a lot of damage . . . damage to your growing body.

Jack   Damage . . .

Mother   Yes, look at yourself. You can't get up in the mornings, you're tired all day, you're moody, you don't wash yourself or change your clothes, you're rude to your sisters and to me.

Beat.

Mother   And we both know why that is. Every time . . . every time you do . . . that, it takes two pints of blood to replace it.

Jack   Blood . . .

Mother *kisses* **Jack**.

Mother   You don't mind me saying this to you, do you?

Jack   No, no.

Mother   One day, when you're twenty-one, you'll thank me for telling you what I've been telling you.

Julie's Bedroom

Julie *and* **Tom** *are playing.*

Enter **Jack***, his hands behind his back.*

Julie   What do you want?

Pause.

Julie   You stink, you know that? You really do stink.

Tom   Stinky.

Pause.

Julie   What do you want?

Jack   Come to get you.

Jack *holds his hands high, fingers spread – he's wearing gloves.*

Tom   Come to get you! Come to get you!

Julie   Where did you, why do you –

Jack   – Father's gardening gloves.

Julie   Get back. You dare. You just dare.

Jack *advances.*

Julie　Mum! Mum, tell Jack!

Jack　Mum's at the hospital.

Jack *advances.*

Julie (*giggles*)　No, no . . .

Jack　Your time has come.

Tom　Time has come!

Jack *grabs* **Julie** *and carries her to the bed.*

Julie　Get away from me.

Jack　They're coming for you. But no one knows where they will strike first.

Jack *tickles* **Julie***, she laughs helplessly.* **Tom** *jumps up and down with excitement.*

Julie　Pl . . . please . . . sto . . .

Jack *keeps tickling.*

Tom　More, more!

Enter **Sue***.*

Sue　What's happening?

Tom　More, more!

Jack *suddenly jumps away from* **Julie***.*

Julie *sits on the bed with her hands between her legs.*

Jack　I'm sorry.

Julie　Get out.

Jack　Sorry.

Julie　Get. Out.

Sue　Let's go to the bathroom.

Julie *exits.* **Sue** *helps her.*

Tom   She's wet the bed!

Jack   Shut up.

Tom   Julie wet the bed!

Jack   I said shut up.

Jack *grabs* **Tom**.

Mother (*off, wearily*)   Hello . . .
I'm back. I need help with dinner.

Dining Room

At the table, **Mother**, **Jack**, **Sue** *and* **Tom**.

Julie *arrives late in clean clothes.*

Mother   There you are Julie. Help your brothers and sister with the table. Make sure the cloth is nice and straight.

Jack *passes a plate to* **Julie***; she ignores him and takes one from* **Sue***.*

They eat.

Mother   It's your birthday in a couple of weeks.

Jack   Yeah.

Mother   Are you excited about being fifteen?

Jack   Dunno.

Mother   My boy, fifteen years old. Why don't we have a little party, that would be nice, wouldn't it? You could invite some friends from school.

Jack   No.

Beat.

Jack   Let's, let's just have the family.

Mother   Yes, just the family.

Beat.

Jack   Pity Dad couldn't be . . .

Mother   Poor dear. He would have been so proud of you.

Silence.

Julie   Eat up, Mum.

Mother   That's what I'm supposed to say.

Sue   It's good stew.

Mother   I'm not hungry . . . can barely keep . . . (*Yawns.*)

Julie   Why don't you have an early night?

Mother   Yes, yes a couple of days in bed and I'll be myself again. Don't you worry, I'll be up in time for your birthday . . . I'm just very, very tired.

Julie   Go on, I'll be up in a minute.

Exit **Mother**.

Julie   Sue, do the washing up will you?

Sue   Okay.

Julie   Jack, empty the rubbish in the bin outside.

Jack   Why should I?

Julie *follows* **Mother**. **Tom** *runs after them.*

Sue   She's changing doctors – I heard her tell Julie.

Beat.

Sue   Do you think she's just sad?

About Dad?

Jack   No, I think they secretly hated each other.

Sue   What?

Jack   And Mum was secretly relieved when Dad died.

Beat.

Sue   You really think?

Julie *re-enters.*

Jack   I think she's happy he's not here any more, and that –

They notice **Julie***.*

Pause.

Julie   Go on, sounds interesting.

Jack   It wasn't anything.

Julie   Oh.

Jack   I was just . . . I was saying I don't think Mum ever really liked Dad.

Julie   Didn't she?

Beat.

Jack   I don't know.

Julie   Don't you?

Jack   Perhaps you know.

Julie   Why should I know?

Pause.

Sue   Because you talk to her more than we do.

Julie   Only because you two won't have anything to do with her.

Exit **Julie***.*

Bathroom

Jack *looking in the mirror.* **Tom** *enters eating a chocolate bar.*

Tom   Happy Birthday to you, squished bananas and stew, you smell like a monkey and look like one too.

Tom *eats more of the chocolate bar.*

Jack   Morning Tom.

Tom   Happy Birthday, Stinky.

Julie and **Sue** *enter.*

Julie *gives* **Jack** *a leather pouch.*

Jack (*excited*)   For my birthday?

Julie *says nothing.*

Jack (*looks inside*)   Nail scissors? And a comb.

Sue   Happy Birthday.

Sue *gives him his present.*

Sue   It's a science fiction novel. See – there's a monster attacking a spaceship on the cover.

Jack   Thanks, Sue.

Jack *shows the novel off to* **Julie**.

Sue   Tom why don't . . . ?

That's not for you, that's . . .

Sue *grabs what's left of the chocolate bar and gives it to* **Jack**.

Tom   Mum gave it me.

Sue   To give to Jack.

Tom   She said it was a present!

Sue   For Jack.

Tom   A present!

Jack   Here, take it.

Tom   Happy Birthday to you! Squished bananas and stew! You smell like a monkey . . .

Julie   We're having the party later in Mum's room. Why don't you do her a favour and clean yourself up for once?

Julie *turns the bath tap on, then shepherds* **Tom** *and* **Sue** *out.*

Jack *waits till they have gone and turns the tap off. He rolls his trouser legs up and stands in the bath and reads the book* **Sue** *gave him.*

Jack (*to* **Older Tom**)   The book Sue gave me – it was the first novel I had read all the way through. The adventures of Commander Hunt.

Enter **Commander Hunt** *from space.*

Com. Hunt   Minute life-bearing spores that are drifting in clouds across galaxies have been touched by special rays from a dying sun.

Jack   What will happen Commander Hunt?

Com. Hunt   They've hatched into a colossal monster that feeds off X-rays and is terrorising regular space traffic between Earth and Mars.

Jack   What will you do about it?

Com. Hunt   We must destroy the beast!

Jack   And let the dead body drift through space for ever.

Com. Hunt   Creating a collision hazard with its gigantic corpse? Don't be foolish. Who knows what other monstrous mutations the cosmic rays might do to its rotten bulk? No, Jack, no.

Jack   I could join the crew and help you explore the galaxy.

Commander Hunt *looks* **Jack** *up and down – he's not impressed.*

Jack   What? I'd be good. I promise.

Commander Hunt *shakes his head.*

Jack   I know I'm only fifteen but I've nearly got a beard!

Com. Hunt   Is that what you call it? Each of the sparse hairs leads the eye, like a pointing finger, to the spot at its base.

Jack   Oh.

Com. Hunt   Start at the top and work your way down.

Jack   I should do my hair like yours?

Com. Hunt   No Jack, no. A man must have his own identity.

Jack   Like this?

Com. Hunt (*laughing*)   Jack, Jack, Jack . . .

Exit **Commander Hunt**.

Jack *takes the leather pouch out of his pocket and uses the comb.*

Jack (*to* **Older Tom**)   I experimented with different styles, deciding at last to celebrate my birthday with a centre parting.

Mother's *Bedroom*

The children arranged around **Mother**'s *bed.*

There is a small cake with one candle.

Family   Happy Birthday to you, Happy Birthday to you, Happy Birthday dear Jack, Happy Birthday to you.

Tom   You're one, you're one. There's only one candle – you're one.

Mother   Happy Birthday, Son. You look smart. Have you had a bath?

Jack   Yes.

Mother *gives* **Jack** *an envelope.*

Jack   Two pounds, thanks Mum.

Jack *gives* **Mother** *a hug – it hurts her.*

Sue *gives* **Jack** *a glass of orange juice.*

Sue   I made it myself from real oranges.

Tom   All oranges are real, aren't they Mum?

They all laugh.

Tom   All oranges are real, aren't they Mum?

Mother   Yes, dear.

Tom   All oranges are real, aren't they Mum?

Silence.

Julie   Tell us your joke, Sue, the one you told me yesterday.

Sue   Why did the man with only one hand cross the road?

Mother   The poor man.

Sue   To get to the second hand shop.

Mother *laughs a little and it fades to silence.*

Julie   Tom, show us your cartwheel.

Tom *cartwheels. Everyone claps.*

Silence.

Julie   Why don't you sing us a song, Jack?

Jack   I don't know any songs.

Julie   What about 'Greensleeves'?

Jack   I don't know it.

Julie   Yes you do, sing it.

Jack   I wish you'd stop telling people what to do. You're not God are you?

Beat.

Sue   Why don't you do something Julie?

Jack   Yeah, you do something for a change.

Julie *suddenly flings herself into a handstand against* **Jack**. **Jack** *holds her legs apart. He looks between her legs. Suddenly:*

Jack   Greensleeves was all my joy!
Greensleeves was my delight,
Greensleeves was my heart of gold,
And who but my lady Greensleeves.

Act Two

Garden

Tom *plays in his sandpit.*

Jack *enters carrying a sledgehammer.*

Jack What are you making?

Tom Houssses.

Jack (*correcting him*) Houses.

Tom Houses. Houses around our house, so our house isn't alone any more.

Jack Oh.

Jack *smashes the sand houses with the sledgehammer.*

Tom *cries and runs off.*

Jack *continues hammering.*

Sue *enters.*

Sue Jack . . . Jack! Jack stop!

Jack *carries on.*

Sue *exits.*

Jack *hammers.*

Julie *enters in a green bikini, carrying a towel.*

Julie You're not to do that.

Jack W . . . why not?

Julie Mum said. Where did you get that hammer?

Jack Dad's shed.

Julie Mum said you're not to do it.

Jack Why?

Julie   She's not feeling well. She's got a headache.

Julie *puts down her towel and lies on it.*

Jack *raises the sledgehammer.*

Jack   When did Mum tell you to tell me to stop making noise?

Julie   Mmmm?

Jack   You were sunbathing out the front before, when did she tell you?

Julie   What?

Jack   I mean –

Julie   – do me a favour, will you, and rub some lotion on my back?

Pause.

Jack *rubs lotion on* **Julie**.

Julie   Up by my shoulders and neck is where it needs it most.

Jack   Th . . . there?

Julie   Mmmm . . . it's your turn to get Tom ready for school tomorrow.

Jack   I did it last time.

Julie   Yeah. Now do my legs.

Jack   Okay.

Jack *looks away as he rubs in the lotion.*

Julie   Careful.

Jack *jumps up and runs away slightly doubled over.*

Julie (*calls*)   Thanks.

Bathroom

Jack *and* **Tom**

Jack   Brush your teeth.

Tom   Don't want to.

Jack   Brush them.

Tom   Not going to!

Jack *shoves* **Tom**.

Jack   Now.

Tom   No.

Jack   It's time for school.

Tom   Don't want to go.

Jack   Why not?

Tom   Because I have an enemy.

Jack   An enemy?

Tom   Yes.

Beat.

Jack   Who?

Tom   A bigger boy out to get me.

Jack   Why?

Tom   Don't know.

Jack   Is it because you're small?

Tom   Maybe.

Jack   Weak?

Tom   He says –

Jack   Jug-eared?

Tom   What's 'jug-eared'?

Jack   When you smile you look like an idiot?

Tom   He says he's going to bash my head in.

Jack   He said what?

Tom   Bash my head in.

Jack   This morning at school, you tell me who he is, you point him out to me, and I'll sort him out.

Tom   He's got friends.

Jack   What does he look like?

Tom   He's got ginger hair.

Jack   I'll sort him out.

With one hand on **Tom**'*s shoulder* **Jack** *strikes a heroic pose.*

Bathroom

All the siblings

Jack *still holds the heroic pose, until:*

Tom *cries in pain.*

Sue   Tom. Tom, what happened?

Tom   I want Mum! I want Mum!

Sue   Oh Tom!

Julie   We can't let Mum see him like this, grab him.

Tom   I want Mum, I want Muuuuum!

Julie *puts her hand over* **Tom**'*s mouth.*

Julie   Shush! Mum's sleeping.

Sue   Our poor little Tom.

Jack   Was it that ginger kid?

Tom   Nooo!

Jack   Who?

Tom (*crying*)   His friends!

Julie *and* **Sue** *wrap a towel round* **Tom**, *wiping him down, whispering to him, hugging and kissing him.*

Jack   He doesn't look so bad now he's cleaned up.

Tom   What's it like being a girl?

Pause.

Sue   It's nice, why?

Tom   I'm tired of being a boy, I want to be a girl now.

Sue   You can't be a girl if you're a boy.

Tom   Yes I can. If I want to, I can.

Julie   Why do you want to be a girl?

Tom   You don't get hit when you're a girl.

Sue   You do sometimes.

Tom   No, no you don't.

Sue   How can you be a girl when everyone knows you're a boy?

Tom   I'll wear a dress and make my hair like yours and go in the girls' entrance.

Sue   You can't do that.

Tom   I want to anyway.

Julie   Poor little thing. We should let him be a girl if he wants to.

Sue   He would look so beautiful in one of my old frocks. That sweet little face!

Jack   He'd look bloody idiotic.

Julie Oh yes? Why do you think that?

Jack You know he would . . . making him look stupid, just so you can have a laugh.

Julie You think girls look idiotic, stupid, daft.

Jack No.

Julie You think it's humiliating to look like a girl because you think it's humiliating to be a girl.

Jack It would be for Tom, to look like a girl.

Sue Girls can wear jeans and cut their hair short and wear shirts and boots.

Julie Because it's okay to be a boy, for girls it's like promotion.

Sue But for a boy to look like a girl . . .

Julie . . . is degrading, according to you, because secretly you believe that being a girl is degrading. Why else would you think it's humiliating for Tom to wear a frock?

Jack Because it is.

Sue But why?

Jack Because –

Julie – if I wore your trousers to school tomorrow and you wore my skirt we'd soon see who had the worse time. Everyone would point at you and laugh. Look at him! He looks just like . . . ugh . . . a –

Sue *and* **Julie**   – a girl!

Sue But look at her, she looks rather –

Julie – *clever* –

Sue – in those trousers.

Julie *and* **Sue** *laugh.*

Jack   You dress Tom up I'll tell Mum.

Tom   My tooth's all wobbly!

Mother's *Bedroom*

Mother *lying in bed,* **Jack** *sits by her.*

Mother   Fed up?

Jack   Yes.

Mother   Let's hope you can find yourself a job in the holidays, get yourself a little pocket money.

Jack   Hmm.

Pause.

Mother   Sit a little nearer, Jack. There's something I want to tell you and I don't want the others to hear.

Jack   Is this about the pints of –

Mother   I might have to go away soon.

Jack   Where?

Mother   To the hospital, to give them a chance to get to the bottom of whatever it is I've got.

Jack (*excited*)   What, for a long time?

Mother   It might be quite a long time. That's why I want to talk to you.

Jack   But how long though, ages?

Mother   It really means that Julie and you will have to be in charge.

Jack   You mean Julie will.

Mother   Both of you. It's not fair to leave it all to her.

Jack   You tell her then, that I'm in charge too.

Mother   The house must be run properly Jack. Tom has to be looked after. You've got to keep things clean and tidy otherwise you know what will happen.

Jack   What?

Mother   They'll come and put Tom in care.

Jack (*excited again*)   Really?

Mother   And perhaps you and Susan too.

Jack   Oh.

Mother   Julie wouldn't stay here by herself. So the house would stand empty, the word would get around and it wouldn't be long before people would be breaking in, taking things, smashing everything up.

And then when I came out of hospital there would be nothing for us all to come back to.

Jack   No.

Mother *tries to touch* **Jack**. *He edges back.*

Mother   I've opened an account at the Post Office for Julie and money will be paid into it from my savings. There's enough for you all for quite a while, easily enough till I come out of hospital.

Mother *sinks back into her bed.*

Jack   When do you go?

Mother   It might not be for a week or two yet, the sooner . . . the sooner the better, I think.

Beat.

Mother   I'm tired of lying around here and doing nothing all day.

Mother *sleeps.*

Pause.

Jack (*to* **Older Tom**)   Three days later our mother was dead.

Living Room

Jack *and* **Julie**

Jack   I want to see her.

Julie   No.

Jack   We're both in charge – she told me.

Julie   She's dead. Sit down. Don't you understand yet? She's dead.

Jack   I'm in charge too.

Julie   She's dead.

Jack   She didn't tell you what she said. I'm in charge too!

Julie   Tom and Sue will be here. We might as well tell them as soon as they get in.

Jack   I don't know, maybe we should . . .

No. Yes. We should.

Silence.

Sue (*off*)   Julie! Mum! Jack! We're home. Tom swam five lengths, didn't you Tom?

Tom (*off*)   Mark Spitz!

Enter **Tom**.

Tom   Mark Spitz! Mark Spitz! My teacher said I was like Mark Spitz!

Silence.

Sue (*off*)   What's for dinner tonight?

Tom   Like Mark Spitz!

Sue (*off*)   I'll drop in on Mum.

Julie *exits*.

Tom   I'm going to play.

Tom *exits.*

Julie *and* **Sue** *enter crying.*

Jack *moves to them and puts his hand on* **Sue**'*s shoulder.*

They do not acknowledge him.

Jack *moves away.*

Tom *re-enters.*

Tom   Who *is* Mark Spitz?

Mother'*s bedroom*

Julie, Sue *and* **Jack** *approach* **Mother**'*s bed.*

Julie   I didn't draw the curtains – to avoid suspicion.

Julie *pulls the sheet up to cover* **Mother**'*s head, which reveals her feet.*

Jack *and* **Sue** *giggle.*

Julie *pulls the sheet down to cover* **Mother**'*s feet only to reveal* **Mother**'*s head.*

All three laugh.

Julie *arranges the sheet so it covers all of* **Mother**.

Sue   It looks ridiculous like that.

Julie   No she doesn't.

Sue *pulls the sheet clear of* **Mother**'*s head.*

Julie (*punching* **Sue** *on the arm*)   Leave it alone!

Enter **Tom**.

Tom   I want Mum.

Julie   She's asleep. Look, you can see.

Tom   Why were you shouting then? She's not asleep, are you Mum?

Sue   She's very asleep.

Pause.

Jack (*to* **Older Tom**)   For a moment it seemed that through sleep, a very deep sleep, we might initiate you in the concept of death. But we knew no more about it than you did, and you sensed something was up.

Tom   Mum!

Tom *grabs hold of* **Mother***'s arm.*

Julie   Come on . . .

Jack   Let him find out for himself.

Julie   You can't, Tom.

Tom   No!

Julie *pulls him,* **Tom** *holds on to* **Mother***, pulling her partially off the bed. Her head strikes the bedside table.*

They all freeze.

Garden

Julie, **Jack**, **Sue** *sit around.* **Tom** *sits apart from them building in the sand.*

Julie   She probably died in her sleep.

Sue   It didn't hurt.

Jack   Are you hungry?

Julie *and* **Sue** *shake their heads.*

Sue   You knew didn't you?

Julie   She's been dying for months.

Jack   What do you mean?

Julie   She didn't want you lot to know.

Jack You lot?

Sue When did you know?

Julie Two weeks before Jack's birthday.

Jack When you did your handstand.

Julie And you sang 'Greensleeves'.

Sue I don't . . . I don't remember what I did.

Pause.

Julie *puts sun lotion on.*

Sue Julie . . . don't you think we ought to tell someone?

Jack If we tell someone . . .

Sue We have to tell someone, so there can be a funeral.

Jack If we tell them, they'll come and put us into care, into an orphanage or something. They might try and get Tom adopted.

Sue They can't do that!

Jack The house will stand empty, people will break in, there'll be nothing left.

Sue But if we don't tell anyone what do we do then?

Jack Word will get around, people will break in and smash everything up.

Julie We can't leave her in the bedroom or she'll start to smell.

Sue That's a terrible thing to say!

Jack You mean we shouldn't tell anybody.

Julie If we don't tell anybody, we've got to do something ourselves, quickly.

Sue But what can we do?

Julie   Bury her, of course.

Sue *cries.*

Jack   Yes, we can have a private funeral, Sue.

Beat.

Jack   Where shall we put her?

Julie   In the garden under the rockery.

Sue *cries louder.* **Julie** *hugs her.*

Jack *sits with* **Tom** *in the sand.*

Tom   Don't smash them.

Jack   I can build things as well.

Tom   I'm building tunnels.

Jack   Your tunnels aren't very strong, they're in the dry sand.

Tom   All sand is dry, isn't it Jack?

Jack   You should build your tunnels in the wet sand so they go deeper, deep under the ground, where the sand is cold and . . .

Tom, go and get me a glass of water will you?

Tom   No, why should I?

Jack *smashes* **Tom***'s tunnels.*

Tom *runs to* **Julie***. Clings to her.*

Julie   Go away. *Please* go away.

Tom   Julie?

Julie   Go!

Tom *runs away.*

Jack   If we bury her here, we'd have to dig deep under the rockery and it would take a long time.

Pause.

Julie   Right.

Jack   If we did it in the day someone would see us, and if we did it at night we would need torches. We might still be seen. And how would we keep it from Tom?

Pause.

Jack (*to* **Older Tom**)   I paused for effect. Despite everything I was enjoying myself. I had always admired the gentleman criminals in films who discussed the perfect murder with elegant detachment.

Pause.

Jack   And of course, if someone came looking, digging up the garden is what they would do first. You read about that sort of thing in the paper every day.

Pause.

Julie   Well then?

Living Room & Cellar

In the living room, **Sue** *curls up in a chair.*

Jack *and* **Julie** *tip the sand from* **Tom***'s sandpit down the coal hole.*

Jack   What will Tom say when he wakes up and finds his sand gone?

Julie (*mimicking* **Tom**)   All blowed away.

In the cellar, **Jack** *and* **Julie** *mix cement and put some in the army chest.*

Mother*'s bedroom*

Jack *and* **Julie**.

Julie   Don't put the light on.

Jack   We can't do it.

Julie   We'll wrap her up in the sheet. It won't be so bad. If we do it quickly, it won't be so bad.

Pause.

Jack   I thought that . . . I can't.

Julie   That's right, leave it all to me. Why don't you do something first?

Jack   Like what?

Julie   Roll her up in the sheet. It's your plan isn't it?

Beat.

Julie   If we spread the sheet out on the floor, we could lift her on to it.

Julie *spreads the sheet out on the floor.*

Jack *rolls* **Mother** *off the bed on to the sheet. He tries to wrap it round her.*

Jack (*crying*)   She won't go. She won't go.

Julie *helps him. They pick* **Mother** *up in the sheet and carry her past:*

Living Room

Sue *in her chair – she watches them.*

Cellar

Jack *and* **Julie** *put* **Mother** *down in front of the chest.*

Sue *joins them.*

All three of them lift **Mother** *into the chest.*

Slowly they throw cement over **Mother***.*

They become more frantic.

Throwing cement on **Mother** *faster, faster and faster.*

Act Three

Sue's *Bedroom*

The children have a massive pillow fight, laughing and jumping and chasing each other around and over the bed.

Sudden stop.

Jack Tom's done a shit in his pants.

Julie Go clean him up then.

Jack Why me?

Sue Because you're a boy.

Jack I'm twelve!

Julie And he's a boy.

Jack You're girls, you should do it.

Tom *cries.*

Julie Lock him in his room.

Sue No.

Julie Tie him to the cot.

Jack Yes, he'll be fine.

Julie Come on!

They carry on with their pillow fight.

Father *and* **Mother** *enter. The children line up in front of them.*

Father Did I not say if the house catches fire you are not to stay and fight it?

The Children The house did not catch fire!

Father Did I not say if someone knocks at the door –

The Children – no one ever knocks at the door!

Father   If someone knocks on the door do not answer it?

The Children   No one knocked!

Father   Did I not say take Tom to the toilet?

Silence from the children.

Mother   He's all right.

Father   But he's covered in . . . that's the last time we go to a funeral.

Father *clips* **Tom** *round the head.*

Father *and* **Mother** *exit.*

Jack (*to* **Older Tom**)   That wonderful afternoon alone all those years ago was no more than a few hours, but the time seemed to occupy a whole stretch of our childhood. In the evening, after dinner, in our pyjamas, we all huddled together in Julie's bedroom and talked of how we would 'do it again' soon.

Kitchen

The kitchen is a complete mess.

Julie *and* **Sue** *are dressing a little girl and giggling.*

Julie   What a pretty little girl.

Tom   It takes a long time, doesn't it?

Sue   Yes, it takes a long time to look beautiful.

Enter **Jack**.

Jack   What are you doing?

Sue   Dressing him up.

Pause.

Jack   What's the point of that?

Sue   Doesn't he look beautiful?

Jack   You shouldn't make him wear that wig.

Tom   It's not a wig, it's my hair.

Jack   It's a stupid wig.

Julie   Oh come on, cheer up, misery.

Julie *ties a ribbon around* **Jack**'s *neck.*

Julie   Here's another one who's tired of being a grumpy boy.

Julie *holds* **Jack**'s *hand. They watch* **Sue** *make adjustments to* **Tom**'s *dress.*

Sue   Isn't he pretty?

Tom *looks down at himself, pulls his dress up.*

Julie (*to* **Jack**)   Now what are we going to do with you, grumpy? You won't make a pretty girl like Tom.

Jack   No.

Julie   Not with horrible spots like those.

Sue   Or with long greasy hair he never washes.

Julie   Or with yellow teeth.

Sue   Or smelly feet.

Tom   Stinky.

Julie   Or with filthy fingernails.

Sue   Look at that one, it's got red and green under it!

Jack (*notices a large cardboard box*)   What's that?

Sue   Ah, that's Julie's.

Jack *opens the cardboard box, pulls out a pair of brown leather boots.*

Jack   Where did you get these?

Julie   In a shop.

Jack   How much?

Julie   Not much.

Sue   Julie! They cost thirty-eight pounds.

Jack   You paid thirty-eight pounds?

Julie   No.

Jack *tries to pull the ribbon off his neck.*

Jack   You nicked them?

Julie *shakes her head.*

Jack   You gave me and Sue two quid each from the Post Office account and you spent thirty-eight pounds on a pair of boots?

Julie   Wrong.

Jack   If you didn't buy them, then you must have nicked them.

Julie   Nope.

Jack   What then?

Julie   Can't you think of another way?

Jack   There isn't another way, unless you made them yourself.

Julie   Hasn't anyone ever given you a present?

Beat.

Jack   Who gave them to you?

Julie   A friend.

Jack   Who though?

Julie   That would be telling . . .

Jack   A bloke.

Jack *tries to pull the ribbon off his neck again.*

Julie   Of course he's a bloke.

Julie *cuts the ribbon around* **Jack***'s neck with scissors.*

Julie   There.

Julie *briefly kisses* **Jack** *on the lips.*

Spaceship/Bathroom

Commander Hunt *and* **Jack**

Com. Hunt   Jack, now that we do not have gravity to keep things in their place.

Jack   Yes, Commander Hunt?

Com. Hunt   We must make an extra effort to be neat.

Jack   Oh.

Com. Hunt   You must give time over to ordering your mind, Jack.

Jack   I will, Commander Hunt, but it's not –

Com. Hunt   – read, and reread, the masterpieces of world literature.

Jack   Okay.

Com. Hunt   And write down your thoughts in a journal, perhaps.

Jack   If you say so.

Com. Hunt   As I do every evening, with my faithful space hound, Cosmo, at my feet.

Jack   I don't have a dog.

Com. Hunt   Your kitchen has become a place of stench and flies.

Jack   I'm not the only one that doesn't do anything about it.

Com. Hunt   A few days ago, someone, *not you*, threw out the rotting corpse of some . . . creature.

Jack   I cleaned out the milk bottles and swatted some flies.

Com. Hunt   Young Jack, do you really think that sufficient?

Jack   There's nothing that could clean it properly.

Com. Hunt   On our space ship, we clean with Earth Rainwater, it's the cleanest water in the universe, we collect it and keep it in large tanks.

Jack   The cleanest in the universe?

Com. Hunt   We go to great lengths to remain hygienic. Think about that.

Jack   Your space ship speeds across the universe at one-hundredth the speed of light. Would you care about the state of the mess room, or about world literature, or writing in journals if your ship remained perfectly still, fixed in outer space?

Silence.

Jack   Well?

Kitchen

Julie *sits smoking.*

Jack   You should read this.

I didn't know you smoked.

Julie   Yes.

Jack   You should read this.

Julie *takes the book.*

Jack   The cover's not much, but it's got some really good things. Commander Hunt –

Julie   – it's not my sort of book.

Jack What do you mean? How do you know what sort of book it is?

Julie I don't feel much like reading anyway.

Jack You would if you started reading this.

Julie All right, if you really want me to, I'll read it.

Jack Don't read it just to please me.

Julie Oh no, of course not.

Jack I'll have it back then.

Julie Maybe I'll read it, when I've got some time.

Jack No, I want it back now.

He grabs her wrist.

Julie You're hurting me.

Jack Give it back. It's not your sort of book.

She lets him take it.

Enter **Sue** *carrying a notebook.*

Jack What's that?

Sue Nothing. Just a book.

Jack What book?

Julie Leave her alone.

Sue Nothing.

Jack *grabs the notebook.*

Jack (*reading*) Tuesday, Dear Mum –

Sue GIVE IT BACK!

Jack *hands the diary back.* **Sue** *storms out.*

Julie What's wrong with you? You ought to be locked up.

Silence.

Julie   Well?

Pause.

Jack   Let's clean up the kitchen.

Pause.

Julie (*an American gangster*)   Now you're talking, brother, really talking.

Julie *stands.*

Julie (*still American*)   C'mon, kid, let's blow this joint sky high . . . huh? HUH?

Jack   Yeah!

Julie (*American*)   It's curtains for this garbage.

Julie *'shoots' the dirty plates.*

Jack   Draw!

Jack *'shoots' at the dirty plates.*

Julie   Oh no! I gotcha!

Julie *pushes* **Jack** *against the sink. She sticks her 'gun' at his throat.*

Julie   Any more trouble from you and I'll stick it in here.

Julie *points the 'gun' at his groin.*

Julie (*whispers*)   Or here.

Enter **Sue**.

Sue   What are you doing?

Beat.

Julie   Sue, you scrub the floor. Jack, you wash the walls. I'm unblocking that drain, wish me luck.

Jack   Aye, aye, Captain!

Julie   Then I'll make a massive stew. We'll have the best dinner we've ever had.

Jack   Sue and I will wash the dishes, won't we Sue?

Beat.

Jack   Won't we Sue?

Beat.

Sue   We're the Ajax Army!

Julie and Jack   White Tornado!

Cellar

Jack *hits a rug with a stick.* **Tom** *carries his Teddy bear.*

Tom (*speaking as Teddy*)   What are you doing that for?

Jack   Getting the dust out. Why are you wearing a skirt?

Tom *ignores him.*

Jack (*to Teddy*)   Why is Tom wearing a skirt?

Tom (*as Teddy*)   Tom is being Julie.

Jack   And who are you?

No reply.

Jack *threatens Teddy.*

Tom   He's being you.

Jack   Did you say me?

Tom '*nods' the Teddy.*

Jack   What do you do in your game?

Tom (*as Teddy*)   Nothing much.

Jack   Do you have fights? Are you friends in your game? Do you hold hands?

Tom *runs off laughing.*

Tom   Hold hands. Hold hands!

Tom *exits.*

Jack *looks at the chest. Leaves the rug. Approaches the chest. Stops.*

Jack   We've, we've cleaned the kitchen up. Sue's set the table for four – she's going to try and get Tom to eat at the table.

Beat.

Jack   Mum?

Pause.

Jack   Did we leave the lid open? I thought I'd closed it.

Jack *looks in the chest.*

Jack   There's a crack in the concrete. It forks at this end.

Pause.

Jack   Can you smell that?

It's weird, almost, sweet.

Probably the stew cooking.

Pause.

Jack   Mum?

If I close my eyes, I can almost see your face.

Say something . . .

Mother   Pass me that book.

Jack   No, that didn't sound like you.

Mother   Good night, Son.

Jack   Those things aren't the sort of things you would say. You were mostly quite quiet, I think. Was your voice low or high? Did you ever make a joke? Are you even in there? I want to hear your voice.

Jack *puts his hands in his pants.*

Mother   Can't you stop drubbing?

Jack   Mother?

Mother   Can't you stop drubbing, even now?

Jack   I'm not doing anything.

Mother   Even while I'm talking to you?

Jack *notices his hand in his pants.*

Jack   I can't stop, it's nothing to do with me.

Mother   What would your father say if he were alive?

Jack   What?

Mother   What would your father say if he were alive?

Jack   But you're both dead!

Enter **Sue**.

Jack *takes his hand out of his pants.*

Sue   I thought that was you down here.

Jack   There's a crack, have you seen it?

Sue   It's getting bigger.

Jack   What should we do about it?

Sue   I don't know.

Pause.

Sue   Guess what? Someone's coming to tea.

Jack   Who?

Sue   Derek. Julie's bloke.

Upstairs, **Derek** *laughs.*

Sue   Listen!

Jack   So what? Big deal.

Sue It's lucky we cleaned up, isn't it?

Jack What's he like?

Sue He's got a car, a new one.

Jack What sort of car?

Sue A red one. It's big. The wheels have silver spokes and the exhaust pipes are silver too. There are long slanting holes along the side of the bonnet.

Jack To let the air in.

Enter **Tom** *in a dress.*

Tom Julie said it's dinner time.

Sue I'm going up to say hello.

Sue *exits.*

Tom Julie said it's dinner time.

Jack What's it like being a girl? Is it better than being a boy?

Tom Dunno.

Jack Does it make you feel sexy?

Tom *laughs.*

Jack Do you understand what I mean?

Tom Sexy.

Jack Well, does it?

Tom I dunno!

Jack When you put your wig on and the skirt, and then you go to the mirror and see a little girl, do you get a nice feeling in your dinky, does it get bigger?

Tom *runs off.*

Julie (*off*) Jack!

Dining Room

Julie, **Sue** *and* **Tom** *are setting the table*. **Jack** *is late*.

Julie There you are Jack. Help your brother and sister with the table. Make sure the cloth is nice and straight.

When we're ready, I'll bring Derek through.

Jack Derek?

Julie I told you he was coming round.

Jack No you didn't.

Julie Are we all ready? Good. Derek! Dinner!

Pause.

Enter **Derek**.

Julie This is Derek. Derek, this is Jack.

Derek *and* **Jack** *shake hands*.

Derek A pleasure to meet you.

Julie This is Tom.

Derek Ah, a Tomgirl.

Sue *laughs*.

Julie And this is Sue.

Derek How do you do?

Sue We really like your car.

Derek Well thank you, yes it is –

Jack I don't like it much.

Beat.

Derek Oh? Why not?

Jack It's too flash.

Julie Sit down, Derek.

They all sit.

Jack   I mean the colour, I don't like red.

Derek   That's too bad. (*To* **Sue**.)   Do you like red?

Sue   Me? Oh, I like red, especially on cars.

Jack   I don't like red on cars. It makes them look like toys.

Julie   Jack can't drive.

Derek   When you're a bit older you'll realise that's all they are: toys, expensive toys.

Jack   Why are they toys? They're very useful for getting about.

Derek   That's true Jack. Very useful. These are big rooms. It's a really big house.

Sue   My room's quite small.

Jack   If cars are toys, then everything you buy is a toy.

Derek   I'll have to think about that one Jack.

Sue   I really like the boots you got Julie.

Derek   Ah, a little present.

Julie   He's incredibly generous.

Jack   If I were you, I wouldn't waste my money on Julie!

No one laughs.

Derek   And what do you want to do when you're grown up, Jack?

Julie   Derek, can you pass me the water?

Derek *reaches for the water.*

Jack   I'll get it.

Jack *tries to beat* **Derek** *to it. He spills the jug on* **Derek**'s *lap.* **Julie** *stifles a laugh.*

Sue   Oh God, Derek, are you okay?

Derek   It's okay, it's okay!

Julie   It was an accident.

Derek   Pot luck. I'll just have to get a towel . . . or something.

Pause.

Julie   I'll show you where the bathroom is.

Derek *and* **Julie** *make to leave.*

Sue   We're really pleased you're here, Derek.

Derek   Thank you for having me, Susan.

Julie   Yes, thank you for coming round.

Derek *touches* **Julie** *on the cheek.*

Beat.

Derek   See you in a jiffy.

Exit **Derek**.

Pause, **Julie** *follows.*

Jack   It was an accident.

Sue   He's got really broad shoulders, hasn't he? He must have had that suit made especially.

Jack   He's not so strong, and he's pretty thick.

Sue   He could beat you up with his little finger.

Jack   Let him try it.

Sue   I bet you can't guess what he does.

Jack   I don't give a fuck what he does.

Sue   You'll never guess. He's a snooker player.

Jack   So what?

Sue   He plays snooker for money. He's incredibly rich. And there was something about him in the paper.

Jack   What paper?

Sue   The local weekly.

Jack   Everyone gets written about in that, if they live long enough.

Sue   I bet you don't know how old he is . . . twenty-three.

Jack   What's so amazing about that?

Sue   It's the perfect age for a bloke.

Jack   What are you talking about? Who said?

Sue   Julie said.

Jack's *Bedroom/Space*

Jack   Commander Hunt?

Are you there?

Commander Hunt?

Act Four

Stairs Landing

A loud radio (playing Rock 'n' Roll music) and a muffled argument can be heard from another room in the house.

Tom, *wearing a dress, sits crying.*

Enter **Jack**. *He immediately smacks* **Tom** *round the head,* **Tom** *screams.*

Enter **Sue**, *diary in hand.*

Sue   What are you doing!?

Jack   It's his own fault, he woke me up.

Sue   Tom, Tom it's all right, ssshh.

Jack   He shouldn't be making a noise like that first thing in the morning.

Sue   First thing! Sssshhh Tom. It's almost one o'clock.

Jack   Well, it's still first thing in the morning for me.

Sue   Quiet Tom.

Jack   What's the point in getting up?

Sue   That's it, Tom, sshh, sshh.

Tom *calms.*

Pause.

Jack   Do you remember when we used to play that game?

Sue   What game?

Jack   When Julie and I were the doctors examining you, and you were from another planet.

Sue   What about it?

Jack   Don't you wish . . . that we still played that game?

Sue   I can hardly remember anything about it.

Jack   Julie and I used to take all your clothes off. Didn't we?

Sue   Did you? I don't really remember it that well, I wasn't very old.

Beat.

Sue   We were always playing silly games.

Pause.

Jack   Don't you ever get tired of reading all day?

Sue   I like reading, and there's nothing else to do.

Jack   There's all kinds of things to do.

Sue   There's nothing else to do.

Jack   You write in that book.

The arguing rises louder than the radio for a moment.

Sue   That'll be them.

Jack   But you still write in that book, don't you?

Sue   A bit.

Jack   I wish you'd let me see the bits about Mum, just those bits. You could read them to me if you like.

The radio is turned up.

Sue   You wouldn't understand any of it.

Jack   Why not?

Sue   You never understood anything about her. You were always horrible to her.

Jack   That's a lie!

Beat.

Jack   That's a lie.

Sue   You never did anything she asked you. You never did anything to help. You were always too full of yourself, just like you are now.

Jack   I wouldn't have dreamt about her then. I dreamt about her and she wanted to know why I'm always drubbing.

Sue   What's 'drubbing'?

Pause.

Sue   Oh. That's not dreaming about her, it's dreaming about yourself. That's why you want to look in my diary, to see if there's anything about you in it.

Jack   Do you go down to the cellar and write about us all in your little black book?

Pause.

Sue *opens her diary.*

Sue   August the ninth . . . you've been dead nineteen days. No one mentioned you today. Jack was in a horrible mood. At lunch we mixed together two tins of soup. Jack did not talk to anyone. Julie talked about her bloke who is called Derek. She said she might bring him home one time and did we mind. I said no. Jack pretended he didn't hear and went upstairs.

Tom *tries to get on* **Sue**'s *lap, she pushes him back.*

Sue *flicks forward a few pages.*

Sue   He has not changed his clothes since you died. He does not wash his hands or anything and he smells horrible. We hate it when he touches a loaf of bread. You can't say anything to him, in case he hits you. He's always about to hit someone, but Julie knows how to deal with him . . .

Sue *snaps the diary shut.*

Sue   Do boys do that all the time, drubbing?

Jack   Julie didn't mention bringing anyone home.

Sue   She did.

Jack   She didn't.

Sue   She did!

Jack   You made it up!

Sue *exits.*

Tom *starts crying again.*

Jack   Why are you crying?

Tom   You hit me!

Jack   Before I hit you?

Tom   Julie hit me and shouted at me.

Tom *cries.*

Kitchen

Derek *and* **Julie**

Radio on loud.

Enter **Jack**.

Derek   Please Julie, be reasonable!

Julie   You should go.

Derek   I only went down –

Julie *turns the radio off.*

Julie   What do you want?

Jack   Just came to see what all the noise was about, and who (*He looks at* **Derek**.) hit Tom?

Pause.

Derek   How are you, Jack?

Julie   Don't.

Derek   What are you up to these days?

Jack   Nothing much.

Beat.

Julie   Derek.

Jack   What about you?

Beat.

Derek   Practising. A few small games. Nothing big, you know . . .

Beat.

Julie   Leave it alone.

Derek   Ever played the game yourself?

Jack   Not really.

Derek   You should come down and have a game.

Beat.

Julie *says nothing.*

Derek   Are you busy now?

Beat.

Julie   Yes, Jack, there's rubbish to . . .

Jack   I'm not all that busy.

Julie *exits.*

Pause.

Derek   Come on then. I'm already late.

Oswald's Snooker Hall

Derek *plays snooker, potting shot after shot. Swaggering around the table.*

Jack *stands apart.*

Derek   Funny set-up in your house.

Jack   I dunno.

Derek   Both parents dead.

Derek *chalks his cue.*

Derek   It's a big house.

Jack   Pretty big.

Derek   Funny smell, though. Have you noticed?

Jack   No.

Derek   It must be worth quite a bit. All those rooms you could turn into flats.

Jack   We're not thinking of that.

Derek   And that cellar, not many houses have a cellar like that.

Jack   Have you been . . . ?

Derek   You could do something with that cellar.

Jack   Like what?

Derek   A snooker table.

Jack   Why do we need a snooker table?

Derek   I could teach you how to play.

Jack   I don't like snooker.

Derek   'Course, you'd need to clear it out. Get rid of the rubbish.

Derek *plays.*

Jack   I'm going now.

Derek   Hang on.

Derek *plays.*

Jack   I'm going back home now.

Derek   You're a queer one. Why don't you relax a bit, why don't you ever smile? You should laugh more you miserable bugger.

Jack   I'm going . . .

Derek   I want to see you laugh.

Jack   I want to go.

Derek   Come on, come on. A big laugh or I'll tell your sister and she'll be mad.

Derek *laughs at Jack.*

Jack   Fuck off!

Jack *wipes his eyes to stop himself from crying.*

Derek   Hey now. Only joking with you. No harm meant me old mate.

Derek *holds out his hand.* **Jack** *doesn't shake it.*

Derek   You're really just like your sister, you are.

Beat.

Derek   Is your sister always like this or is there something wrong I should know about?

Jack   Always like what?

Derek   Strictly man to man, you understand?

Jack   Yes.

Derek   Take this afternoon for instance. She was doing something, so I thought I'd take a look round your cellar. No harm in that. But she got very funny about it. I mean, there's nothing funny down there is there?

Jack *doesn't respond.*

Derek   Is there?

Jack   No, no, I hardly ever go down there, but there's nothing.

Derek   So why should she get so upset?

Jack   She's always like that. That is what Julie is like.

Derek   And another time –

Jack   – I really have to go now.

They look at each other.

Derek   What you four need is taking care of.

Julie's *Bedroom*

Jack, **Julie** *and* **Tom**.

The cot from the cellar is now in **Julie**'s *room.*

Tom *sits in the cot sucking his thumb. He has a bib round his neck. One side of the cot is down.*

Julie   Enjoy your game?

Jack   What is Tom –

Julie   – don't be surprised. Don't be surprised. Tom wants to be a little baby.

Tom *sucks his thumb loudly.*

Julie   He was such a naughty boy this afternoon so we had a long talk and decided lots of things.

Julie *hums quietly to* **Tom**. **Tom** *lies down and sleeps.*

Jack   Why didn't you put the cot in his own room?

Julie   My sweet little boy wanted it in here.

Julie *kisses* **Tom** *and raises the side of the cot.*

Julie (*softly*)   There's a good boy.

Julie *takes* **Jack**'s *hand and leads him out.*

Bathroom

Jack *alone*

Jack (*to* **Older Tom**)   I began to notice a smell on my hands. It was sweet and faintly rotten and was more on the fingers than the palms, or perhaps even between the fingers. It was a smell that reminded me of the meat we had thrown out.

Enter **Commander Hunt**.

Jack *combs his hair.*

Jack (*to* **Older Tom**)   I took long baths in the middle of the afternoon and lay perfectly still without a thought until the soapy water was cold. I cut my nails and washed my hair.

Com. Hunt   I am proud of you, Jack. Keep this up and one day you too will have a starship and be able to leave this world. You'll journey to the furthest corners of the universe.

Jack   I stopped masturbating.

Com. Hunt   Good for you, Jack, good for you.

Jack *sniffs his hand.*

Jack   But the smell . . .

Com. Hunt   Yes?

Jack   It comes back.

Com. Hunt   Ah.

Jack   After each bath it comes back, distant, more like a memory than a smell, but it's always there.

Com. Hunt   Perhaps you have been contaminated.

Jack   You mean with the . . . ?

Com. Hunt   The spores, you have been contaminated with the spores from deep space.

Jack   What will happen to me?

Com. Hunt   I do not know, Jack.

Jack   Commander Hunt?

Com. Hunt   I do not know.

Exit **Commander Hunt**.

Enter **Julie** *in a bathrobe.*

Jack   What will happen to . . . (*Notices* **Julie**.) what?

Julie *presents* **Jack** *with a plastic bag.*

Julie   They're for you.

Jack   A present?

Julie   From a jumble sale.

Jack *puts on a shirt.*

Jack   A good fit.

Julie   Nearly new.

Jack   Thank you.

Julie *begins to button up the shirt.*

Julie   So who is she?

Jack   Who's who?

Julie   The girl?

Jack   What girl?

Julie   The one you're washing your hair and cutting your nails for?

Jack   There isn't –

Julie   She must be special.

Jack   I haven't, there isn't a girl.

Julie   Is she a secret?

Jack   No.

Julie   It's okay, we all have secrets.

Jack   I don't know what you're talking about.

Julie   All finished. You look very smart.

Jack   Do you think I have cancer?

Julie *laughs.*

Jack   How do you know? I could be rotting away from some disease. Inside.

Julie   Don't be silly.

Jack   I could be, there is this smell . . .

Julie   I hope your girlfriend likes the shirt I got you.

Jack   I don't have a girlfriend.

Julie *starts to take her bathrobe off, stops.*

Jack   I don't have a girlfriend.

Julie *waits for* **Jack** *to leave.*

Jack *leaves, smelling his hands as he goes.*

Garden

Jack *alone. It is raining.*

Jack   I don't have a girlfriend.

Jack *takes off his clothes and steps into the rain.*

Sue *(from inside)*   What are you doing! Come inside!

Jack   It's Earth Rainwater, the cleanest water in the universe!

Jack *stands in the rain, arms outstretched.*

Sue   Come inside!

Jack   It's the first time it's rained since Mother died.

Sue   It's rained loads of times!

Jack   Prove it.

Sue   I've used my umbrella, it's in my room.

Jack   That's no proof at all.

Sue   You prove it hasn't.

Jack (*shouting*)   I don't need to, I know!

Julie's Bedroom

Julie *and* **Tom**

Tom *in the big brass cot.*

Julie   There was such a commotion,
  That little Jenny wren
  Flew down into the garden,
  And put it back again.

Enter **Jack**, *sopping wet.*

Tom   Go away, you go away!

Jack   You go away! Why are you in bed? It's not even seven!

Julie   What am I going to do with the two of you?

Tom, Jack just wants to kiss you goodnight, too. Don't you, Jack?

Jack   Real babies kick and scream when they get put to bed.

Tom   No they don't. Not always they don't.

Julie *kisses* **Tom** *goodnight.*

Pause.

Jack *kisses* **Tom** *goodnight.*

Tom *settles down to sleep.*

Jack *and* **Julie** *sit on the bed.*

Julie   You're soaking.

Jack   Perhaps it's bad for Tom to go on pretending to be a baby.

Julie   Bad? Why?

Jack   Perhaps he won't be able to come out of it.

Julie *puts her hand on* **Jack***'s knee.*

Julie   I think someone is jealous.

He touches her back.

Julie   Do you think a lot about Mum?

Jack   Yes, do you?

Julie   Of course.

Pause.

Jack   Do you think what we did was right?

Julie *takes her hand from* **Jack***'s knee.*

Julie   It seemed obvious then, but I don't know now. Perhaps we shouldn't have.

Jack   We can't do anything about it now.

He runs his finger up her spine.

Julie   No, I suppose not.

Jack   You let Derek into the cellar.

Julie *stands.*

Julie   Is that what he told you when you were playing . . . billiards?

Jack   I only watched.

Julie   He found the key and went down there to look around.

Jack   You should have stopped him.

Julie   He just took the key. There is nothing to see down there.

Jack   You got really angry about it and now he wants to know why.

Beat.

Julie   You know, I haven't slept with him or anything.

Exit **Julie**.

Jack (*calling*)   So what!

Enter **Sue**.

Sue   That smell's back.

Jack *smells his hands.*

Sue   Come on.

Cellar

Sue *and* **Jack**

Sue   Come on!

Jack   Quiet.

Sue   I know what that smell is.

Jack   It isn't me.

Sue   Go on, you'll see.

They both hold a hand over their noses.

Sue   Uoook.

Jack   What?

Sue *takes her hand away.*

Sue   Look.

Jack *hesitates.*

Sue (*whispering*)   What are you waiting for!

Jack *doesn't look. Shakes his head.*

Enter **Commander Hunt**. **Sue** *takes on the appearance of SOOOSAN the alien.*

Com. Hunt   We have encountered a barren planet. Nothing but thousands of miles of hard-baked desert.

Sue   You know what it is. Did you see? Through the crack.

Jack *hesitates to look in the trunk.*

Com. Hunt   Do not be frightened by my alien companion, Jack. Sooosan is an archivist from the planet Issacius. She records all my daring adventures in the ship's log.

Sue   The sheet is all torn.

Com. Hunt   Look, Jack, look.

Jack   I don't want to.

Com. Hunt   Afraid?

Jack   I don't want –

Com. Hunt   Look.

Jack *looks in the trunk.*

Sue   You can see her –

Jack   – her nightie.

Com. Hunt   Earthquakes are opening up great fissures across the planet's surface.

Jack   It's almost as if she's still . . .

Sue   Almost.

Jack   The smell, it's –

Com. Hunt   – yes Jack.

Jack, I fear the time has come. I must leave this planet.

Jack   But Commander Hunt, no.

Com. Hunt   You must adventure on alone, dear boy. And I, I must return to the stars.

Commander Hunt *fades away.*

Jack *continues looking into the trunk.*

Jack (*to* **Older Tom**)   It was of course the same smell, but it was changed by being intensified. Now it was separate from me. There was something sweet, and beyond that, or wrapped around it, another bigger, softer smell that was like a fat finger pushing into the back of my throat.

Sue   We'll have to get more cement.

Enter **Derek**, *carrying his coat.*

Derek   What have you got down here that smells so good?

Pause.

Derek   Sorry.

Sue   It's the drain.

Derek   It's a very odd smell.

Sue   It's the drain outside the kitchen. It gets blocked very easily and in the summer . . . you know . . . it's the drain.

Derek   The drain?

Sue   Yes.

Jack   Where's Julie?

Derek   Checking on Tom.

Jack   He sleeps in her bedroom now.

Derek   He's an odd one your little brother, isn't he? I mean putting on girls' dresses . . .

Jack   What's odd about that?

Sue   Do you think?

Derek   It could affect him later in life you know.

Jack   What do you mean by that?

Derek   I mean, when did your parents die exactly?

Jack   Long time ago.

Derek   Julie told me it was recently.

Enter **Julie**.

Julie   All very quiet.

Derek   We were talking about the drains.

Derek *holds out his arm for* **Julie**, *but she stands by* **Jack**.

Julie   Drains?

Sue   Let me take your coat.

Derek *cradles the coat in his arms, strokes it.*

Derek   Nice pussy.

Pause – no one laughs.

Derek   It was a joke.

Sue   Is Tom okay?

Julie   Quiet as a mouse.

Derek   A bit early isn't it? For Tom?

Julie   In fact, it's a bit later than usual, isn't it, Jack?

Jack   Yes.

Julie   Haven't you noticed a difference in him?

Derek   Cleaner and smarter.

Julie   A handsome young man.

Derek   Yes.

Julie   Still pale, though. He really ought to get out in the sun.

Derek   Pulling the ladies now are you, Jack?

Julie   Oh no, we're having none of that round here.

Derek *laughs. A delay, then* **Sue** *laughs.*

Julie   Let's go upstairs, this smell is getting on my nerves.

Derek   But you haven't told me what it is yet.

Jack   It's none of your business really.

Derek   It's just, I'm curious. Curious.

Derek *looks into the chest.*

Derek   Whatever's in there is really rotten.

Julie   It's a dead dog. Jack's dog.

Jack   You promised you wouldn't say.

Julie   It doesn't matter now.

It's his idea of a . . . a tomb. He put her in there when she died and poured concrete all over her.

Derek   Oh. You didn't make a very good job of the mix.

Julie   The smell is all over the house, Jack. You'd better do something about it.

Derek   I think it calls for a re-burial, in the garden, perhaps?

Jack   I don't want it moved. Not after all that work.

Beat.

Derek   So, what's this dog called?

Jack   Cosmo.

Derek   *Cosmo?*

Julie   Cosmo.

Derek   We'll have to seal that crack with cement then, and hope that stops the smell. I'll show you how to make a proper mix this time.

Act Five

Garden

Julie *sunbathing in her green bikini.* **Tom** *playing around her.*

Jack *watches from a distance, unseen.*

Tom   Julie, watch! Julie! Julie, look. Look I can jump right over it. Look.

Julie   Well done, Tom, well done.

Tom   And look, look, I can run all the way round the garden in ten seconds. Look.

Tom *runs.*

Tom   Onetwothreefourfivesixseveneightnineten.

Julie   Tom's our champ!

Come here you've got ice cream round your mouth.

She wipes his mouth.

Tom   Ice cream round my mouth.

Jack   Wotcha.

Tom   Gonna build castles. On my own.

Jack   Let's hope they don't fall down.

Julie   You look so weak. What have you been doing with yourself?

Beat.

Jack *and* **Julie** *laugh together.*

Jack   You should be careful. The radio said it's the hottest day since 1900.

Julie   My skin is used to it.

Jack   You'll be black tomorrow.

Julie   You are so pale.

Why don't you stay out in the sun?

With me.

Jack *takes off his shirt and lies down next to* **Julie**. *They sunbathe in silence.*

Tom watches them together. **Tom** *starts crying.*

Julie   What is it?

Tom   My finger! My finger!

Julie   My little baby. Let's get you a magic plaster.

Tom   A mag . . . magic plaster?

Jack   I'll help.

Julie   It's okay, you need some sun.

Exit **Julie** *and* **Tom**.

Jack *sleeps.*

Jack (*to* **Older Tom**)   I woke up as the sun started to go down and wondered why I was not in my bed. I stood up too quickly and my head began to ache. I stared for a while at my reflection in the kitchen window. I admired the blood-red colour of my chest and arms, deepened by the evening sunlight.

Off – **Derek**'s *laughter.*

Cellar

Enter **Jack**, *his shirt in his hand.*

Derek *is repairing the crack in the cement with a trowel.* **Julie** *watching.*

Derek   Hello Jack! Doing your chores for you.

Jack   The smell's better.

Julie   Look at you, you've really caught it. You look lovely. Doesn't he look lovely?

Derek *works.*

Derek   Quite the picture of health.

Standing behind **Derek**, **Jack** *pretends to kick him in the backside.* **Julie** *and* **Jack** *giggle.* **Derek** *turns.*

Derek   Anything wrong?

Julie   No, no.

Jack   No, nothing.

They giggle.

Derek (*to* **Jack**)   Perhaps you'd better do it.

Jack   Oh no, you're much better at it than I am.

Derek   No, no Jack, it's your dog, after all. You ought to.

If it *is* a dog.

Julie   Derek (*Touches his arm.*), please do it. You said you would. If Jack does it, it will only crack again and the smell will be everywhere.

Derek   I've done the mix now, he'd be fine with it.

Julie   Please.

Derek *continues working.*

Julie (*softly*)   Nice pussy.

Jack *and* **Julie** *giggle again.* **Derek** *ignores them.*

Derek *works.*

Derek   Finished.

Julie   Well done!

Derek *tries to hold* **Julie**'s *hand, but she moves over to* **Jack**.

Julie (*to* **Jack**)   You look so much better, doesn't he?

Derek Looks like he overdid it to me.

Julie Oh no, just right.

Derek Jack. You must have been very attached to that dog.

Jack Yes.

Derek When did he die?

Jack It was a she.

Derek Well, when did she die?

Jack About two months ago.

Derek Julie . . . ?

Julie Two months ago.

Beat.

Derek What kind of dog?

Julie Oh you know, a mixture of things.

Jack But mostly Labrador.

(*to* **Older Tom**) And briefly, from somewhere, a dog seemed to lift its sunken eyes to mine.

Derek Do you mind talking about it?

Jack No.

Derek Why put her down here?

Jack Sort of like preserving her. Like the Egyptians.

Enter **Tom**.

Tom I'm hungry!

Derek Tom! Did you like Cosmo?

Tom *hides behind* **Julie***'s legs. Sucks his thumb.*

Julie You remember Cosmo, our dog.

Tom Cosmo.

Derek   Yes, Cosmo. Were you sad when she died?

Tom   Cosmo?

Julie   You sat on my lap and cried, don't you remember?

Beat.

Tom   Yes . . . I cried, didn't I?

Julie   That's right and I carried you to bed, remember?

Pause.

Tom   A dog!

Julie *chases* **Tom** *out, they exit.*

Derek *looks at his watch.*

Jack   Golden Labrador.

Derek   I've got a game. (*Calls.*) Julie, I've got a game! (*To* **Jack**.) See you later tonight perhaps.

Derek *goes to exit.*

Derek   I wish you would all . . . well, trust me a little more.

Darkness.

Crying.

Julie's *Bedroom*

Tom *is crying.*

Jack   Wotcha.

Tom *cries.*

Jack   What's wrong with you? Why don't you shut up?

Tom *cries louder.*

Jack   Wait.

Jack *tries to lower the side of the cot. Fails. Hits it with his fist.*
Tom *laughs.*

Tom   Again! I want you to do that again!

Jack *tries again to lower the side of the cot, hits it again.*

Tom   Why haven't you got any clothes on?

Jack   I was sleeping in my room. I got hot.

Tom   I'm hot too.

Jack   Was that why you were crying? Because you were hot?

Tom   Yes.

Jack   Crying makes you hotter.

Tom   I wanted Julie to come up. She said she would come up and see me.

Jack   Why did you want her to come up?

Tom   Because I wanted her to.

Jack   But why?

Tom   Because I *wanted* her.

Jack   Do you remember Mum? Don't you want her?

Tom   She's dead.

Jack *climbs into the cot.*

Jack   Even though she's dead don't you wish she would come up and see you instead of Julie?

Tom   I've been in her room. I know where Julie keeps the key.

Jack   What do you do in there?

Tom   Nothing.

Jack   What's in there?

Tom   Julie put everything away. All Mum's things.

Jack   What did you want with Mum's things? Did you play with her things?

Tom   We did dressing up and things.

Jack   You and Julie.

Tom   Me and Teddy, stupid!

Jack   You dressed up in Mum's clothes?

Tom   Sometimes we were Mummy and Daddy and sometimes we were Julie and you and sometimes we were Julie and Derek.

Jack   What did you do when you were me and Julie? I mean . . . what did you do?

Tom   Just play.

Jack (*to* **Older Tom**)   Because of the way the light was on your face, and because you had secrets, you seemed like a tiny, wise old man lying at my feet. I wondered if you believed in heaven.

Do you know where Mum is now?

Tom   In the cellar.

Jack   What do you mean?

Tom   In the cellar. In the trunk under all that stuff.

Jack   Who told you that?

Tom   Derek said. He said you put her there.

Jack   When did he tell you that? What else did Derek say?

Tom   He said you keep pretending it's a dog! A dog!

Jack *laughs.* **Tom** *is sleepy.*

Jack   Tom. Tom. Why do you want to be a baby?

Tom   You're squashing me, you are. You're squashing me and it's my bed . . . you . . . (*Yawns.*) you . . .

Tom *sleeps.*

Jack   Goodnight Tom.

Jack *kisses* **Tom** *on the forehead.*

Julie *enters.*

Julie   Look at you.

Jack   Julie, I, just . . .

Julie   Just look at you! Two bare babies!

She strokes **Jack**'*s head.*

Julie   You sweet little thing.

Jack *raises his thumb to his mouth. Stops.*

Julie   Go on, don't be afraid.

Puts his thumb in his mouth.

Beat.

Jack   I'm getting out.

Julie   Look! It's big!

Jack *jumps out of the cot.*

Julie   Don't go away yet. I want to talk to you.

You look lovely without your clothes, all pink and white like an ice cream. Is it sore?

Jack   No. What about your clothes?

Julie *undresses.*

Julie   What do you think of Tom? Do you think he's happy?

Jack   Yes.

Pause.

Jack   He said that Derek told him about what's in the cellar.

Julie   Derek's known for ages. We haven't been very good at keeping it a secret.

What upsets him is that we don't let him in on it. He feels left out when we go on telling him it's a dog. He wants to be one of the family, you know, big smart daddy.

He's getting on my nerves.

Jack *touches* **Julie** *on her arm.*

Jack   Since he knows we might as well tell him. I feel a bit daft going on about that dog.

They hold hands.

Julie   He takes charge of everything. He keeps talking about moving in with us. 'What you four need is taking care of.'

Pause.

Julie   He lives with his mum in this tiny house. I've been there. She calls him Doodle and makes him wash his hands before tea.

She puts her hands on either side of his face.

Julie   She told me she irons fifteen shirts a week for him.

Jack   That's a lot.

She squashes his face in so that it looks like a bird's beak.

Julie   You used to look like this all the time, and now (*She relaxes her hold.*) you look like this.

Jack   You haven't done any running for a long time.

Julie   Perhaps I'll do some in the winter.

Jack   Are you going back to school next week?

Julie   No. Are you?

Jack   No.

They hug.

Julie   It's funny, I've lost all sense of time. It feels like it's always been like this. I can't really remember how it used to be when Mum was alive and I can't really imagine anything changing.

Everything seems still and fixed and it makes me feel that I'm not frightened of anything.

Jack   Except for the times I go down into the cellar I feel like I'm asleep. Whole weeks go by without me noticing, and if you ask me what happened three days ago I wouldn't be able to tell you.

Julie   What if someone knocked down our house, what would happen?

Jack   Someone would come poking around and there'd be nothing left. All they would find would be a few broken bricks in the long grass.

Julie   It wouldn't matter. Would it?

Enter **Derek**, *unseen.*

Julie *moves* **Jack**'s *head to her breast.*

Jack   Julie.

Julie   Go on.

Jack   Julie.

Julie   Go on.

Jack *sucks* **Julie**'s *nipple.*

Pause.

Derek   Now I've seen it all.

Julie   Have you? Oh dear.

Derek   How long has this been going on?

Julie   Ages. Ages and ages.

Derek   All those times . . . you never even let me come near you.

Pause.

Derek   You could have just told me.

Julie   Actually, it is none of your business.

Derek   If you'd have told me I would have cleared off, left you to it.

Julie   Typical! That's typical!

Derek   It's sick, Julie. He's your brother.

Julie   Talk quietly, Derek, or you'll wake Tom up.

Derek (*quietly*)   Sick. All of you.

Sick.

Exit **Derek**.

Jack *blows a raspberry on* **Julie**'*s breast.*

Julie *puts her hand on* **Jack**'*s belly.*

Julie   Look how white you are, against my hand.

Jack   Look how small your hand is, against my hand.

Both (*comparing hands*)   Hands.

Both (*comparing ears*)   Ears.

Both (*comparing tongues*)   Tongues.

Both (*comparing belly buttons*)   Belly buttons.

Both (*comparing legs*)   Legs.

Both (*comparing knees*)   Knees.

Both (*comparing shoulders*)   Shoulders.

Both (*comparing hair*)   Hair.

Both (*comparing backs*)   Backs.

Both (*comparing bums*)   Bums.

Both (*comparing arms*)   Arms.

Both (*comparing necks*)   Necks.

Both (*comparing heads*)   Heads.

Jack   Teeth.

Julie   Mouth. (*Laughing.*) Breasts.

Julie *straddles* **Jack**.

Jack (*to* **Older Tom**)   Julie took hold of my penis and pulled it into her. There was something soft in my way and as I grew larger inside her it parted and I was deep inside.

Julie *leans forward and kisses* **Jack**.

Julie   It's easy.

Jack (*to* **Older Tom**)   I sat up a little way and pressed my face into her breasts. She took a nipple between her fingers again and found my mouth.

A rhythmic thudding shakes the house.

Jack *and* **Julie** *move in time with the rhythm.*

Jack (*to* **Older Tom**)   I listened to my sister's beating heart, and felt my heart keeping time, and all there was, was the slow unending pulse.

Julie   It's time to turn over.

His leg gets caught under hers. They try to roll one way and almost fall off the bed. **Jack** *pins* **Julie**'s *hair with his elbow.*

Julie   Ouch!

The couple giggle and lie next to each other. They forget what they're about.

They listen to the thudding. It stops.

Silence.

Enter **Sue**.

Sue He smashed it up! Derek found the sledgehammer and he smashed it up.

But he's gone away now.

A long silence.

The following section is spoken to **Older Tom**.

Jack For a long time no one spoke then we seemed to wake up and talk in whispers about Mum.

We talked about her illness . . .

Julie And what it was like when we carried her down the stairs.

Sue And when you tried to get in bed with her.

Jack I reminded them about the day of the pillow fight when we were left in the house together.

Julie I had completely forgotten it.

Sue So had I.

Julie We reminded Jack of a holiday in the country before you were born.

Sue Julie and I discussed what Mum would have thought of Derek.

All She would have sent him packing!

Jack And that woke you up.

Sue We talked about the birthday party at Mum's bedside and Julie's handstand.

Jack How her dark, brown limbs had barely quivered and how Sue and I had wanted to applaud.

Older Tom We talked about how there were blue flashing lights outside. And what that meant. We talked about the voices in the house and how I mustn't be afraid. We talked about Mum and Dad.

Julie asked me if I had had a lovely sleep.

I remember, I had.

End.

DRAMA ONLINE

A new way to study drama

From curriculum classics
to contemporary writing
Accompanied by
theory and practice

Discover. Read.
Study. Perform.

Find out more:
www.dramaonlinelibrary.com

 FOLLOW US ON TWITTER @DRAMAONLINELIB

 BLOOMSBURY

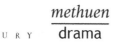 *methuen*
drama

 THE ARDEN SHAKESPEARE

 FABER DIGITAL

Bloomsbury Methuen Drama Modern Plays
include work by

Bola Agbaje
Edward Albee
Davey Anderson
Jean Anouilh
John Arden
Peter Barnes
Sebastian Barry
Alistair Beaton
Brendan Behan
Edward Bond
William Boyd
Bertolt Brecht
Howard Brenton
Amelia Bullmore
Anthony Burgess
Leo Butler
Jim Cartwright
Lolita Chakrabarti
Caryl Churchill
Lucinda Coxon
Curious Directive
Nick Darke
Shelagh Delaney
Ishy Din
Claire Dowie
David Edgar
David Eldridge
Dario Fo
Michael Frayn
John Godber
Paul Godfrey
James Graham
David Greig
John Guare
Mark Haddon
Peter Handke
David Harrower
Jonathan Harvey
Iain Heggie

Robert Holman
Caroline Horton
Terry Johnson
Sarah Kane
Barrie Keeffe
Doug Lucie
Anders Lustgarten
David Mamet
Patrick Marber
Martin McDonagh
Arthur Miller
D. C. Moore
Tom Murphy
Phyllis Nagy
Anthony Neilson
Peter Nichols
Joe Orton
Joe Penhall
Luigi Pirandello
Stephen Poliakoff
Lucy Prebble
Peter Quilter
Mark Ravenhill
Philip Ridley
Willy Russell
Jean-Paul Sartre
Sam Shepard
Martin Sherman
Wole Soyinka
Simon Stephens
Peter Straughan
Kate Tempest
Theatre Workshop
Judy Upton
Timberlake Wertenbaker
Roy Williams
Snoo Wilson
Frances Ya-Chu Cowhig
Benjamin Zephaniah

For a complete catalogue
of Bloomsbury Methuen Drama
titles write to:

Bloomsbury Methuen Drama
Bloomsbury Publishing Plc
50 Bedford Square
London WC1B 3DP

or you can visit our website at:
www.bloomsbury.com/drama

Made in the USA
Las Vegas, NV
30 October 2022

58443575R10059